Jews

Poems
Translations from Hebrew
1982-2013

Sami Shalom Chetrit

Červená Barva Press
Somerville, Massachusetts

Červená Barva Press
P.O. Box 440357
W. Somerville, MA 02144-3222

www.cervenabarvapress.com

Cover Art: Igal Fedida: "A painter without words." water on canvas, 2014. http://www.igalfedida.com

Cover Design: William J. Kelle

Author Photo: Shlomit Carmeli

Production: Mikail Jaikaran

Bookstore: www.thelostbookshelf.com

Library of Congress Control Number: 2014957560

Translation from Hebrew:
Ammiel Alcalay
Dena Shunra
Shay Yishayahu Sayar

Translation editor
Ammiel Alcalay

Book editor:
Fred Dewey

TABLE OF CONTENTS

III. Poems in Ashdodian

IV. A Distant Proverb

V. And Only Love

I'm a *Gotta Move* Jew

I'm on the move.
I came yesterday – tomorrow I'll go.
You won't catch me pouring down foundations.
My roots of memory longing
like my tailbone to the cut-off tail.
I move and move, turn quickly,
turn upon the ground,
not rooted, not hovering
I will not stay to age in people
and the people will not age in me.
Here is one fall and spring
and it's already stifling here.
Gotta move on
let me through
                                I need some air.

Jews

Poems
Translations from Hebrew
1982-2013

I. A Mural With No Wall

A Mural with No Wall
A Qasida for Mahmoud Darwish[1]

It's been a while that I've wanted to write to you, not about you,
And even now I don't know where to start, from where
I can take words to face your eternal words, and I am in transit
Through the verse-houses of your poems, homeland of the words,
folded into slim volume – cities
Of poetry which – I'll be frank with you – fill me with envy
recently;
Not that of a poet but of an exile: it is so yours, so fully yours,
I have no such homeland, neither in writing nor on earth
But do not pity me – that's not it. When it comes down to it,
I am the murderer
And a thousand petitions against the occupation won't help me,
I am the soldier
Who kills three pigeons again and again with a single shot
And it is a matter of habit –
It was me who shot the forsaken horse, alone beside the house that
became my new home
And I who sealed its windows well against the keening of the
yearning mourners
And I who sealed the well with armored concrete
That I should not see nor hear life from within the water
And what do I need an Arab horse or eternal Sabra cactus for?
You will find not even one Sabra cactus to soothe your soul
in the sand dunes of Isdud[2]
Where we built a city for people who have never heard your name
Your name rubbed out in Moroccan and in Russian and in
Ashdodian[3] Hebrew,
To tell you the truth, Andalusia or not,

---

[1]   Mahmud Darwish is the most renowned Palestinian national
      poet.
[2]   The Palestinian village of Isdud was occupied and destroyed
      by Israel in 1948. The residents were made refugees.
[3]   The Israeli city of Ashdod was founded approximately at the
      site of the demolished village Isdud. Immigrants flown in from
      Morocco (1950s-1960s) and from Russia (1970s-1990s) were
      settled there. It became renowned for being a "development
      town", although it's the fifth biggest city in Israel.

That's how we do Andalusia in Ashdod, among the Jews,
And now they celebrate fifty years for it in a brand-new museum
by the sea, exactly at the spot where
Nabi Younes, a fishing village, used to stand; and the exhibition
holds
Not even one shred of lonely Arab horses and no Sabras
And children are taught the ancient history of the city
The Philistine, not the Palestinian, because museums are not about
politics.
I read your poems as indictments and plead guilty to every single
charge,
Each time anew, and my thousands of protests will not help here,
against the elders of Zionism,
Nor the youngest, Ashkenazim and Mizrahim, white and black –
I am one of them
Because I am not one of you, that is the miserable bottom line;
I – who steals in and out of your thresholds as if it were my own -
Sipping from the Arab coffee,
Kicking at the jug and shouting 'dirty Arab!'
Smashing each and every mirror so that I will not see in them
The face of my grandfather, puzzling back at me, in Arabic.
What do you mean Arabic? I am a Hebrew poet!
I am a jailor-poet, do not believe a word I say,
I am the jailor of myself and of my words
Whose wings are clipped, and of my sleep that wanders,
With no exact address to rest within,
And you were so right – the homeland is not a suitcase;
And you were so right – the homeland is a suitcase,
As the Jews can explain at the airport, you there!
What are you flying with the whole homeland in your
suspicious suitcase?
That's the most basic irresponsibility, step aside please, I
The security screener dressed up as a Middle Eastern intellectual
Desperately seeking his homeland inside an Arab suitcase,
And me, all the words of love and agony that I have written and
that I have yet to write and also all those
That beat against my temples, that I will never write,
Even they will never be salvation for me and for you
As in my life I embody your death,
You are suffocated because I breathe,

You are hungry because I eat,
You are bound because I am unfettered,
Write it down,
Your shackles are my wings
And how am I to write you words of peace, of coexistence, *ya'ani*
ta'ayush[4],
Even if I buy myself a suitcase just like yours and travel far away
from here,
And I have traveled so, so far away from here, and it does not go
away, this thing,
As an Arab intellectual once told me with a madman's bluntness:
"How can you insist on being with the Jews?"
I laughed at him, what do you mean, how? I am a Jew, I do not
know how to be something else,
What insolence! I am a Jew, not a Zionist but a Jew, I have been a
Jew since the dawn of the Mugrabi man,
And perhaps I did not really understand until my son grew up and
became a lad who reads for himself and hears things on his own...
And one day, when I told him sadly how far he is going from us,
from the Jews, he shook me off politely:
"What do you want from me? You said get up, we have to go to
America to run away from the Hebron Jew,
But you can't, because there are no other Jews in the
world... you are running away from yourself, Dad."
And I sat and wept bitterly; I so envy his freedom,
I so would like to take leave of my knowledge, my mind, my
consciousness...
And so, dear Arab poet, I write to you in Hebrew,
And so, painter of eternal words, I paint for you in Jewish,
A mural I have no wall for, nor will I ever,
As I have come to detest your land and my land has always cast me
out,
And I live in exile on motes of air, not here nor there,
Closing my eyes, touching, not touching...
Look,
How you fall asleep and the Jew inside me creeps up with words
To make you feel guilty, to wheedle compassion out of you,

---

[4]   *Ya'ani* is Arabic for "in other words." *Ta'ayus* is Arabic for
        coexistence.

And Ecclesiastes and all of his vanity of vanities will not help you here,
Nor will the Song of Songs, nor the poetry of poetries,
Even the Messiah himself will not save you from me and me from you,
Because I have killed him this morning,
I rise every day to kill him anew,
To put off the end of everything,
For on this day atonement shall be made for you...
For on this day he shall rise above the fear of heights and depths
And he will come a-running to me on the waves of the roiling bog,
On this day the worlds will be upturned and then I will stand
Before my grandfather and my son and look them in the eye and say Enough!
The tapestry of my life is Jewish lies in Arabic embroidery,
And it is not that I took your life and made it mine,
But rather your life was once your life until King David came from Poland
And knocked us both down with just one sling shot,
As if we were the eyes of that same Goliath,
A single Polish shot did us both in,
As we were busy with prayers and storytelling, baking bread and cracking olives,
And other time-consuming, mind-sweetening, Arab activities of the heart,
But the King desired me and raised me up
To life, like Elisha, with a single vodka-filled blow, and sent me upon you,
Sent me free and cried: The Arab is dead! The Arab is dead! Long live the new Jew!
Write it down,
I was born Jewish out of your death, the death of the Arab in me,
And then we danced a bracing Hora and the Polack brandishes my grandfather's beard
And points at my dark skin and sings: Here is where I came from, this is where I hail from, this is my home!

And I was filled with new Jewish pride and sharp wolves' teeth and
you – *rooh min houn*[5]! Go away!
You refused to remove yourself from my eyes, watching to the
Western horizon...
You became my enemy, who peeks anew at me from the mirror
every morning,
And I spit and curse and kill you and kill you again,
To rebirth myself a renovated Jew,
And do not mistake me, I am not here to replace you,
I am not an Orientalist, I am Oriental, *ya'ani* a *Mizrahi* Jew,
There is no atonement or redemption for me, not in this lifetime,
Perhaps on the day that your three companions overcome their
fear of heights,
Lo,' those inquirers into the secret of life –
Gilgamesh, Solomon, and Yeshua[6] (Jesus, King of the Jews) –
And descend from the top branches of the tree of life down to the
land of the end of all,
On that day, which will nevermore come,
I will tear the mask off my face,
Benevolent of countenance and soul,
And be who I am,
Whoever I am I will be,
A Jew with no Jews,
An Arab with no Arabs,
A suitcase with no homeland,
A homeland with no suitcase,
A painter with no words,
A poet with no paint,
A wall with no mural,
A mural with no wall.

---

5   *Rooh min houn* is an Arabic phrase known to most Israelis. It
means "go away from here," and it's used broadly by soldiers
toward Palestinians.

6   *Yeshua* is one of the Hebrew forms for the name Jesus. Many
Jews refuse even to mention this form.

My Mother Loves Arik Sharon

My mother loves Ariel Sharon,
that's what she tells me,
now that he's dying in the endless broadcasts
(the endless talk of intracranial hemorrhages and edemas
gives her a headache, she should only be well),
and me, I love my mother, that's the thing,
even now, while he does his dying, all over the downer evening
line-up
(Really, it makes me ill, zap to a soap Mother).
I'll also love my mother after that,
when they'll have dedicated a hall of culture to him,
across the street from her,
and we'll go there together, to hear an Andalusian concert.
"Poor thing, he didn't deserve that," says my mother, sadly
(dead prime ministers always make her sad, even Ben-Gurion,
certainly Begin).
And I love my mother, that's the thing,
and how can I heap ashes on her sorrow
(now is not the time to remind her how he took me all the way to
Beirut, for instance, and how she showered him with curses then,
but does she need that, now, during the national celebration of
broadcast grief?)
Ye'ebi bashk ubashna aiyma.
May his soul be your redemption and ours, Mother.

Ashdod, 1.6.06, 3:35pm

I am an Arab Refugee

When I hear Fairuz sing:
I will never forget you, Filasteen,
I swear to you by my own right hand
that at once I am a Palestinian,
I suddenly know:
I am an Arab refugee.
If I'm not,
let my tongue dry up and fall free.

Talking to an American Zionistomat

The Jew-from-Here has long since become a Zionistomat
With a built in, hard-burned dictionary FAQ in his head
And he is ever CampusWatchful night and day
And ever sings the songs and has their say...
And you can activate him with keywords.
You can say:
"The Refugees"
And he'll shoot back at you in a blink of GoogleSpeed:
They rose up to destroy us / their leaders told them to run away /
They have twenty-two states and we have only one and /
What do they know about refugees, anyway? / We are all refugees,
/
six million dead / A Jew has nowhere to go - ...
And he is fifth generation American
Two generations of being a proud Zionistomat,
He votes for Bush and the Terminator
Axis of Evil
War against Terror
Toss out the immigrants
Hasta la vista, baby.
I propose
"A State for all its citizens"
And the Zionistomat spews
Arab majority / destruction of the State of Israel / Holocaust /
six million dead / Only a self-hating Jew could... / danger... /
enemy...
Calm down, I try to speak. I meant America.
Ah, America, he smiles, and slides out of automatic speech,
That's a whole 'nother story.
The democratic rationale rules here, freedom for all.
And the Indians? I try to discuss.
They have reservations – what's wrong with that? he winks.
And the blacks? I say.
Anyone who wants to succeed – does – he shoots back at me.
Look: Powel, Rice, Oprah, Thomas...
Ok, ok, I say. But what about all the rest?
The rest – he raises his voice and suddenly becomes another
automat, a local one:

They should go study / they should stop shooting each other / they should go work / they should stop making babies / My great-grandfather came here with one dollar in his pocket and never asked a thing from anyone / They should stop whining / enough with this talk about all that slavery and discrimination and all that bullshit … /

I've had enough, as well. I turned away from him, nauseous, and he called after me with a final, non-automatic cry,

Tell me something, if you're such a humanist,

how come the Jews don't shoot anyone, huh?

Show me where a Jew can walk around with so much hate and so many weapons…

The Jew in Hebron

The Jew in Hebron,
who is the Jew in Hebron?
What is the Jew in Hebron?
Why is the Jew in Hebron?
Shut up, you! I didn't ask you!
Don't you give me fables now.
Your forefathers that you pray to
would give you up for adoption,
for treatment or hospitalization,
but really, those forefathers of yours,
the forefathers you pray to, are not really
YOUR forefathers, to tell the truth, I mean,
If we pull out the documents and pedigrees
as you like to declare, in other words,
show me your genealogy, not a covenant of blood and soil.

Speedy Jew

His name is Speedy
And his boyish smile captures your heart
He flies a Cobra; thirty-six years old;
So sweet, he loves his work, his country (what else),
Has nothing on his mind beyond the mission, he says, beyond the
target.
They call him – and he comes.
He is a gentle man, perhaps a gourmet. He was a chef in New
York, oh yeah.
And now he imports wines.
At least, in his civilian life.
(I've always wanted to ask what this nonsense is about some
civilian life? Do they think we're stupid?)
He loves the ejaculated adrenaline, in the kitchen as in the Cobra
head
What's most important is to get it right, to smash a target as you
spice a dish,
That's how he testifies to the work of his hands (say, a bleeding
steak done rare and reddish wine)
His buddies have called him Speedy since his days at air force
school
He is quick, reacts like lightning, has neutralized all thought and
feeling
(He left those, well, back in civilian life, this afternoon)
Think what you may think, say what you may say,
You will never be prepared enough. You will fall in love with this
guy in an instant,
He loves his wife just like the Cobra,
Glance at him and his smile will melt away any wicked thought,
If you had one,
About a proud, Jewish Cobra pilot,
A speedy Jew,
Look at him a moment longer: his upright posture, helmet and
insignia,
Caressing the warhead as though it were a bottle of fine
Chardonnay.
Look at him, his fingers fluttering over the rudder,
Ahhhh, it melts your heart. Just another moment,

Just another turn, another gentle pull,
Ahhhh, just another moment, if you have it,
A thump, a bump,
....and the red smell,
Intoxicating,
Like wine,
Like blood.

They Can Give it All Back

We came as far as America
so that our son could learn in a public school
about cowboys and Indians and Spanish priests
who came to save the soul of the red man and the textbooks
they have some political corrections in them –
The cowboys are a little bad now and the Indians
get a little white pity – but the kid knows clearly
who the pioneers were and who discovered whom and
who built what and how.
When I was his age I learned American history at the movies.
How I loved to see John Wayne shoot down those Apaches
from the mountain passes, one hand shooting, the other holding
the reins,
and a girl clutching him from behind, shrieking with every shot.
That's why I wasn't really surprised, years later, when I read
about the extermination of the millions of Indians. It was clear to
me since forever.
After all, I had learned about it back at the neighborhood movie
house.

So I'm a pest, and I want to politically correct the lesson even more
so I tell my young son "you should know that the white men
hunted down the Indians and killed at least twenty million and
every step you take in America
is on stolen Indian land."

And little him, he is appalled, looking for a way out:
"I didn't steal anything, Abba!
As far as I'm concerned, they can give it all back."
We came as far as America
To hear the purest truth:
To give it all back.
In your dreams.

A Man Seeks Roots

Lovingly dedicated to Yiram Attiya's* mother

A man seeks a root in a flagpole
and axes the roots of his forefathers.
He plants himself in the land of fear and denial
sending his branches out to grab black clouds of glory.
A man erases his father and mother and draws himself as the flag,
waving in the winds of war and contention.
A man finds a root
and he is a pole
and a flag.

* Yiram Attiya is a young Israeli man who declared that he has Hebraized his Jewish-Moroccan family name, Attiya, into Netanyahu, because he was horrified when he was at a clinic waiting room one day, and ran into an Arab woman who bore the same family name as he did, Attiya. Here is how he expressed his horror in the Maariv Newspaper, 20 October 2005: "'Mrs. Attiya,' I said to myself, and thought that in another situation, I could even think this was my mother... ...everyone, every single person and there should be no exceptions, should Hebraize their family names and connect with their true roots – the holy language. As I have done."

Red Kite
For Mordechai Vanunu

A Little girl flies a red kite
on the beach
in North Korea.
In a moment the kite will melt
and the string
and the hand
and the girl will melt
and the beach in North Korea will melt.

And possibly,
a little girl flies a blue kite
on a barren hill
in Dimona.*

Dimona is a little town in the Negev Desert, near Israel's main nuclear facility.

Thus Spake the Lord

The Lord came to me in my dream
And thus spake the Lord
God of Sarah and Hagar
God of Ishmael and Isaac
God of the Pieces
God of the Covenant
God of man
God of blood
The God of thy seed as the stars of the heaven
The God of as the sand which is upon the sea shore
The God of the ashes at the bottom of the Danube,
Thus spake the Lord God of Zion and Falasteen
The god of stupid, dead soldier Yitzhak,
The God of the checkpoint baby who will not be born
Thus spake the Lord to me, in Modern Hebrew:

Tell 'em I've had it;
I've lost my patience;
The special status has expired.
The covenant is oh-vuh!
You are in breach of contract. I'm fed up.
Neither chosen people nor first born
Tell them in their own Hebrew:
You've become a shitty people,
A people of shit.

There. I've said it.
Thus spake the Lord.

An Answer for the Agents of Freedom

Choked
my soul is choking
there is not one place left
in the expanse of this globe
to which you can run to be free,
even in America they're looking for America
in this global village, as the globals like
to call this concrete and asphalt monster,
sliced and diced and blotted
everywhere from the heart of the driest desert to the furthest icy
steppes
the guard will always pop up in front of you,
from out of nowhere, and all your freedom
suddenly shrinks into his holster
and all you can do is pull out a guitar
and sing a song for freedom
and love and peace and you can get high
and imagine your hair and hers
blowing in the wind
on a green country road into forever
that becomes real
in the boots
of the next
guard
or the fence
or the thirst
and the poem.
For what?

The Jews Are Killing the Savior

The Jews killed the Savior
this morning.
The Jews kill the Savior
every day anew
and it is a matter of habit and tradition.

The Jews kill their savior,
the breath of their soul, to strike a covenant
with the suffering of the flesh forever.

Rag Poem

I brought a rag with me, to America,
a fine cotton mopping rag
that sops up water and squeezes out just right,
also a big black rubber squeegee just for the tiles.
That's how I like to do the floors in America
(well, not like those good old tile floors in the projects back home).

Now I can hang my special rag to dry, and sigh,
And say aloud, just like we used to say back there:
You can't walk there, children! The floor is wet!
And the longing is easier, mopped clean.

Get Thee

Listen well my son, to your father's teachings:
Fuck well,
eat well,
and see the world.
Get up, get thee from thy father's house and thy mother's house
get thee from one homeland to another
to any country that you lay your eyes upon
and do not dally with the flag-wavers,
do not read with the sanctifiers of books
do not put your faith in gun-sellers
they're soul-merchants, one and all,
send them to hell.
Tell them to go fuck themselves.
Them, and their sons and grandsons.
Listen well, my son, to your father's teachings:
Don't look to the side roads, beware,
that's where the fixers of the world naively cry -
their fiery eyes have forever singed my soul –
but you, beware. Keep away from them.
Take yourself a woman
she'll take you for her man.
Don't make her swear by your mother's gospel,
don't believe her father's creed
because love is your only faith.

Make yourselves a home.
Give her a son.
She will give you a daughter.
Teach them how to get up
teach them how to walk
teach them to get up and walk away
teach them long-distant marching
tell them some story to remember,
sing them some song for their spirit,
play a tune for their heart
under the tree in the yard.
That's all the good there is, my son.
And there is nothing more beyond it.

Washing the Car

When the weight of the world's vanities
breaks your spirit's back,
I mean, when the shit backs up your soul,
I recommend abstinence from book reading
or holding conversations of any significance
or cooking up goal-oriented thoughts.
Go wash the car
scrub it like it were your soul
and if you haven't got a car
go mop the floor.
And if you haven't got a floor
nor even a faucet
then start shouting.
Shout wordlessly
don't mean a thing
lest you end up with a poem.

Measurements

En route to a seminar on political poetry at Berkeley U.,
I saw two engineering students
measure distances and slopes,
imagining another bridge to run here
and beneath it another railway there
another so and so glass towers,
and who cares what –
They measure practical things
while I am on my way to measure meanings
of oblique poems
in an ancient contentious language.
You can bet I felt like shit.

It was only after two hours of measuring,
deconstructing Nathan Zach,*
that I thought:
Those two will miss
. these bad ol' days
when tomorrow's bad ol' days arrive.

*Israeli Poet.

In Lieu of Curses

Prayers that we say
on the way down into the void,
In lieu of the curses
In our bursting belly,
Very soon,
like children in the dark
quelling demons with
whistles and whispers
not to get so crazy-scared
not to shout
Mommmy…

Because it is actually broad daylight
and there are no demons here
and we have long since not been children,
and so the land is not a bad one
only its rulers that are bloodied
and a void is the vision of its future.

We've Already Seen This Movie

We've already been in this movie, I mean
we've seen it at least once before, in other words
not that we, ourselves, were there in this movie,
the one that's happening to us now
on a screen of earth and skies,
where in the third act their boundary line will blur
In a stupendous red and orange fire, and clouds of smoke
will cover everything. But we'll appear before that,
in the second act, where soldiers of Truth and Eternity come by
to load us up into trucks, best case,
which means they'll shoot the others on the spot, before our eyes,
and then appoint new writers, teachers, judges upon us
to wash away our sins and so on,
as on this day Your Sins Shall Be Washed Away, et cetera,
and we watch, amazed, and say – we've already been in this movie,
meaning, we ourselves haven't really,
In other words, soon,
in a moment, they'll turn out the light,
and we'll see.

Stupid Sheep in Sesame Sauce

Pompous compilers of religious books will write one day
About Ariel Sharon (the son of Tatar farmers, head of the Zionist state,
Governor of all Palestine, and so it goes, all over them)
In the book of their Third Destruction, and they will say he was
Sent by the God of Raging Morals to be the punishment
Of the sinning nation of Israel, who oppositionally bang their headses into wallses.
But how did the Sages say? Their very head of state, duly elected, was their heavy sin
Their sin born again and again from putrid depths of stupidity,
Not an oops-I-really-didn't-notice stupidity,
Not some sort of passing distraction (like a little war in the northern parts or bombing a city of Philistines),
But actual stupidity, such that the holy souls of the Israeli public
Went stupider and stupider until they could no longer be salvaged
Other than by penalty of the man of flesh, who would sacrifice flocks of them
As if they were not, Israelis, children of the first man, in His image,
And even if the children of Israel, sons of that Adam and the sweat of his brow,
What does all this fancy talk matter –
There goes all the Divinity and Knowledge blown into them by the Creator, quacking out of their throats,
As if they were bleating sheep, jumping fools, lost in the desert, among the sycamores

Blessed Be She

The Jews here – some among them pray:
"Blessed be Our Lady, Our Goddess, Queen of the universe,
Creator of the fruit of the vine."
OK, I'm kind of starting to like it. Or now, at least,
after the first shock and whiplash,
Blessed Be She and Blessed Be Her Name forever more
Amen – Amen. Really, from the heart.
Because that's not it at all.
What the Hell does it matter
to the nutters in His land or Hers?
To the holy Messiahs or Messiaesses
who desecrate His image or Hers?
What in tarnation does it matter
if His or Her sons spill the blood
in His name or in Hers?
No one will go and check to see
if it will be He or Her making peace
in His heavens or in Her heavens.
Really, She should just get on with making it, He should...
They should make it together, One Body,
in Her name, in His name,
twice, with love.
Amen.

Who Is A Jew And What Kind Of A Jew He Is?

1. The Story is Told:

An American Jew dies and he leaves no children.
In his will, the following is written:
"I hereby decree that all my money and property
be given over to the State of Israel and my last
wish is that I be buried in the Land of Israel.
The undersigned, Isaac Cohen."
The attendants sent the deceased and his money,
according to his last request, to the Land of Israel,
to eternal rest. The clerks of Zion collected
his money and transferred the corpse, as a matter
of course, to the burial society of the Ashkenazi Jews.
They turned his papers upside-down but found no authorization
to determine whether or not he really was an Ashkenazi.
Because of their doubts they deferred, sending him
on to the eternal resting place for Sephardic Jews.
The Sephardic sages sat down to take the matter
under advisement and, in conclusion, their answer
was formulated like this: "The name Isaac Cohen could
be either here or there, and given that this is so,
if he is a Sephardic Jew, then we have been privileged
to fulfill a wonderful commandment; and if he is
an Ashkenazi Jew, then we will gladly bury him!"

2. Getting to Know a Friendly American Jewish woman: Conversation

Tell me, you're from Israel?
Yes, I'm from there.
Oh, and where in Israel do you live?
Jerusalem. For the last few years I've lived there.
Oh, Jerusalem is such a beautiful city.
Yes, of course, a beautiful city.
And do you...you're from West...or East...
That's a tough question, depends on who's drawing the map.
You're funny, and do you, I mean, do you speak Hebrew?
Yes, of course.

I mean, that's your mother tongue?
Not really. My mother's tongue is Arabic, but now she speaks
Hebrew fine.
Oh, 'Ze Yofi,' I learned that in the kibbutz.
Not bad at all.
And you are, I mean, you're Israeli, right?
Yes, of course.
Your family is observant?
Pretty much.
Do they keep the Sabbath?
Me, no, depends, actually...
Do you eat pork?
No, that, no.
Excuse me for prying, but I just have to ask you, are you Jewish or
Arab?
I'm an Arab Jew.
You're funny.
No, I'm quite serious.
Arab Jew? I've never heard of that.
It's simple: Just the way you say you're an American Jew. Here, try
to say "European Jews."
European Jews.
Now, say "Arab Jews."
You can't compare, "European Jews" is something else.
How come?
Because "Jew" just doesn't go with "Arab," it just doesn't go. It
doesn't even sound right.
Depends on your ear.
Look, I've got nothing against Arabs. I even have friends who are
Arabs, but how can you say "Arab Jew" when all the Arabs want is
to destroy the Jews?
And how can you say "European Jew" when the Europeans have
already destroyed the Jews?

3. When I Left

It was only when I left that I remembered
I hadn't wanted to get so involved,
I really only wanted to tell her
that my first babysitter in Morocco was a Muslim girl

36

and that I have a black-and-white photo of her in an old album
sitting on the mosaic tiles in the courtyard
and that when I was a new Moroccan stiletto immigrant
I tried in vain to recall a little boy's conversation
with his babysitter in Moroccan Arabic.
And whenever we brought her up, my mother would say:
How she loved you, she never left you for a second.

My Love, My Land

Don't go from me spare my heart that is torn
between you and her, this damned one
That I love so much and do not know why
for my feet indeed step
upon her bleeding claws.
In the name of my love for you
please wait,
for soon they'll destroy everything of her
and again we will set out beyond the seas
if the heart endures until then
if you should endure, you in your battered love
over ancient strands of land,
grasping it with your ten fingers
and I pray for you and for her the wretched one
whose ears are shut to the song of conquerors,
to the silent elegy of the oppressed.
Don't flee from me,
Look how meager she is
and meager her inhabitants
and meager their prayer
and there is no love in her.
Love is not in her.

Binding

God knew that Abraham knows
that God knows that he knows
that God knows that Abraham knows.

Abraham knew that God knows
that Abraham knows that he knows
that Abraham knows that God knows.

And the sacrificial lamb?

Letter to the Bearers of the Dead

They bear their dead in the light
and sing *Yet Our Father Lives*.
They bear the dead and at times
it seems that the dead bear the living
and the dead do not sing,
what do the dead care if our father yet lives,
what do the dead care about darkness or light,
if they are carried along avenues
or in dark alleys.

For the dead are dead and you
only the flesh do you bear,
the soul is no longer within your hand's reach
and the truth must be spoken –
You have no true claim to God.

They bear the motionless *block* of flesh
and call it faith, *Emunim*.
They stuff the earth with their children
and claim our children too,
for the sacrifice is never enough.
But we see that they have no angel
and they have no ram in the thicket,
they know this well
and God knows better than they.

II. War is a Lousy Time

Hey Jeep, Hey Jeep

1. Eight boys in an army jeep
    eight soldiers, one major
    eight boys and one minor

2. *Hey Jeep, Hey Jeep,*

3. And his son Ishmael was thirteen years old
    at the cutting of his uncircumcized flesh.

4. And eight of his sons in the army jeep
    and his son cries to the Lord but no one hears

5. And behold his father running:
    Run, Muhammad, run,
    your son's spirit is coming towards you

6. Lord, Lord: where is the lamb for a burnt offering?

7. Now these are the generations of Ishmael, Abraham's son,
    whom
    Hagar the Egyptian, Sarah's handmaid, bore unto
    Abraham;
    And these are the names of the sons of Ishmael,
    by their names, according to their generations:
    the first-born of Ishmael, Nebaioth; and Kedar, and
    Abdeel, and Mibsam, and Mishma, and   Dumah, and
    Massa, Hadad, and Teman, Jetur, Naphish and Kedemah
    ... and Muhammad Said Qarada
    and Said Qarada whose years numbered thirteen at his
    death.

8. And these are the generations of Isaac, Abraham's son:
    Abraham begot Isaac; and Isaac begot Esau and Jacob;
    now the sons of Jacob were twelve in number; the sons of
    Leah:

Reuben – Jacob's first-born - Simeon, Levi, Judah,
Issachar, and Zebulun;
the sons of Rachel; Joseph and Benjamin;
and the sons of Bilha Rachel's handmaid: Dan and
Naftali;
and the sons of Zilpah, Leah's maid: Gad and Asher;
these are the sons of Jacob who were born to him in
Paddan-Aram

9. And eight soldiers in an army jeep.
    One has officer's stripes on his shoulder,
    A Hebrew officer to the Kingdom of Israel:
    Maybe a bleeding-heart liberal
    Or a down-and-out reactionary.

10. *Hey jeep, Hey jeep,*
    what a night it is!

11. Maybe his name's Itsik

12. And the seven under him:
    One's and eagle eye
    Another bound to ritual
    The third has his fit on the ground
    The fourth's got his head in the clouds
    the fifth's got to do it all
    the sixth replies stoically
    the seventh can't wait for liberty

13. And there are "dovish intellectuals" amongst them,
    and there are "militant hawks" amongst them,
    and God is there amongst them,
    and an officer is there amongst them.

14. soon there's neither,
    affection nor innocence

15. Black combat boots on their feet:
    "that oppress the poor and crush the destitute"

16. Subject displayed the following signs:
     pallor, bleeding from the nose and left ear.
     Internal hemorrhaging in the vicinity of the left temple.
     Compound fractures resulting from a blow
     (not a projectile), on the left temple.
     Break in the left knee.

17. He was thirteen the day of his murder.

18. Thirteen: the age of Bar-Mitzvah.

19. Theater of the struggle:
     As one they arose and came from the
     combines and the collective farms
     from the shareholder's settlements
     and the surroundings, from the towns and from the cities.

20. *Take her to the left a bit,*
     take her to the right.

21. And the boy cried to his father: Father, I'm choking!

22. Eight pairs of heavy duty combat boots

23. Eight outstretched pairs
     and there were white amongst them
     and there were black amongst them.

24. *Hey Jeep, Hey Jeep*

25. Eight soldiers, one a Hebrew major
     eight soldiers, and one Arab minor.

26. *Hey, everyone agrees: with a jeep*
     the only thing you need is speed,

27. They finally pitched him from the fleeting coach,
     cast their spirit to the blinding night.

28. *Like wind up in the sky*

we'll fly
                right on by

29. but thou shalt love thy neighbor as thyself
     but thou shalt love thy neighbor as thyself
     but thou shalt love thy neighbor as thyself
     but thou shalt love thy neighbor as thyself
     but thou shalt love thy neighbor as thyself
     but thou shalt love thy neighbor as thyself
     but thou shalt love thy neighbor as thyself
     but thou shalt love thy neighbor as thyself
     but thou shalt love thy neighbor as thyself
     but thou shalt love thy neighbor as thyself
     but thou shalt love thy neighbor as thyself
     but thou shalt love thy neighbor as thyself
     but thou shalt love thy neighbor as thyself

                              Jerusalem, December 31, 1988

New Jerusalem

Bad Dream, Part 1:
The state, unlike an individual, has no conscience.

—George Kennan

A wild night,
Someone turned me to the gourds.
Scrambling through the forest of concrete and glass towers,
They're here, they are there, everywhere,
Riding on black horses and waving truncheons
Calling out to me halt in Hebrew and I do not wonder,
As they get closer I see my Hebrew teacher,
The justice from the Rabbinate and one respected professor
Wearing an American cowboy hat.
The rest are in state uniforms.
I was caught like a rat in the corner of a dark alley.
(Shots in the air, sirens whining.)
Stop, password! The old justice cries to me.
The lord is God, I exclaim in tears
and the professor shoots the justice dead and berates me:
God has nothing to do with it! You have screwed us!
And the Hebrew teacher corrects, one should say 'let us down,'
my esteemed professor.
He shoots her dead too and aims at me and fires…
and fires… and fires
I wake up in horror, damn it,
the television's still on (one should say 'is still on'),
American cops loading the body of a young black guy
into a flashing ambulance.
A tall man in a cowboy hat reveals the face of the deceased,
for a moment, lights a cigarette and hisses through a jet smoke:
"He was stubborn, stupid son of a bitch."
Limping to the bathroom, sweating, pissing out
all my dreamy fear.
I turn the T.V. off and fall back asleep.

Nightmare, [bad dream] Part 2:

Here's the sign: "New Jerusalem," down in the dark city.
I break an opening through the wall and cross over to its Eastern
side.
A woman in Arab garb whose face is the face of my mother and
my grandmother,
calms my crying on her shoulders,
You just had a bad dream. You're home now.
No! I scream. They've got state uniforms
and truncheons and guns and they have no conscience,
they're shooting at rabbis and teachers.
Believe me, I saw it with my own teary eyes.
We got to the village, they washed my face and served me
goat milk, black olives and warm bread.
The milk is from your goat, my mother says,
we bought her for you when you were two,
so you would grow and flourish and let go of my weary breasts.
I give my speech in the village center
Before an indifferent crowd:
Two old women, my mother, my grandmother,
Two venerable old men in shiny *galabiyas*,
A plentiful cow, a sleepy donkey and a lame dog.
I remember the closing sentence:
There is no New Jerusalem, it is all vanity,
I saw it with my own eyes, just a sign in the wall,
don't follow them, they're all cops.
The cops appeared from over the hills
led by a man in a cowboy hat.
They built me a gallows from fine wood,
I smoked one last American cigarette,
they put the rope around my neck
and the professor reads my indictment and my sentence,
repeating and emphasizing: you screwed us! You screwed us…
And then suddenly from the sky a ball of fire dives towards me
and lo what a wonder - my son, riding a rocket of fire
scorches the rope and pulls me on high:
Hold on tight, daddy, I'm the Rocket Man…

I woke up smiling to the morning sun,
on my back is mounted my busybody son
shouting into my ear:
Daddy, hold on tight! I'm the Rocket Man,
I'm taking you to Jerusalem…

How Shall We Say Lo, How?

How did we sit to the side.
And not alone we sat
And not like the blind in the courtyards.

Lo, the eyes
they are wide open,
but the arms
are crossed like a statue of clay
and the faces
resemble those of the saints
until the storm passes
as if it is not ours.

In other words:
Sticking one's finger down
the throat of the news,
to throw up one's visions
making room for a good movie.
Like this, until the storm passes
as if the storm is not ours.

And how shall we say lo, how.
How did we sit to the side
thinking the roof would not come down
on us all.

Midnight atop the Regional Garbage Dumpster

In two bands on this side and that
with drawn swords
their eyes in flames,
and at their leads two big rogues,
atop the regional garbage dumpster.
Between them one centimeter of terror,
announcing in loud voices
the camps are ready for war.

And I mewl to the cats in their language:
What have I got with you, rogues,
bastards,
let me dump out my garbage
And you, go ahead,
dump your blood, fighting
over the regional garbage dumpster.

Acrid Memory

At the train station a rabid crowd
Doles out yellow ribbons and flags
asking passersby to pledge their blessings
and give thanks to the boys coming home.
As for me, I put down:
miserable, pitiful souls.
And a stinging memory comes back.
Homecoming memory.
Driving through the streets of a strange city at full tilt
(the streets there weren't at all unfamiliar to us),
an old Arab stood by the side of the main road waving his cane
(now I think: that old man's grandfather once must have stood
by the side of that very road and waved that very cane).
We stopped to find the meaning of his wave.
The old man bent toward me (in his eyes I saw that he didn't
get the essence of human adulation,
the quality of victory or failure), and spit a yellow
glob of saliva in my face before turning back on his way.
And on that day I was purified.
If only for a fleeting moment was I purified.

1991

"And Thou Shalt Teach Them Diligently to They Children"

I am teaching my son to play soccer
in a strange land
I diligently teach my son soccer
in the land of baseball
I bring up my son in soccer
the way we used to over there.

Me and my son
kick back and forth to each other in Hebrew
I'm cautious and weary
he's tough and quick on his feet.

Kicking a soccer ball
back and forth
as we remember Zion.

Like a Turtle

I've seen turtles seven hundred years old
and there are old elephants that look like trees
that look like stones with which walls were once raised
and there are stones that no man has touched for eternities.

Soldiers are falling hundreds and thousands of years
and live only twenty
(and see, for example
the father's dreams
and the mother's nightmares
and the woman,
ask the meaning of her cries),
and we don't count the years of the stone
the one lie over the heart,
or the one laid over him,
like a turtle.

Victory Parade

There's a victory parade on Broadway for the
glorious heroes: routers of the Middle Eastern devil.
And tucked away in the corner of the paper is a picture
of a woman from that demonic country: her piercing eyes
bore into God's focused lens, from her hands she offers
her shriveled-up child as he swallows up the scene
with silence and an abbreviated gesture.
In small print, the headline reads:
A helpless Iraqi mother bears the corpse of her dead baby.

Song of Ascent for Mordechai

A song of ascent for Mordechai
in his ascension over truth's pavilion
crying out a vision for the end of all flesh
sounding the alarm over the evil to come
ringing bells of fire.

A song of ascent for Mordechai
for whose tidings
he was pitched into the cistern
as befits a prophet of truth.

A song of ascent for Mordechai,
my brother my brother Mordechai
your outcry is too heavy to bear,
but behold, your light wings
carry me
over the mountains of pitch,
where the Prince's vile hand
can't touch us.

A song of ascent for Mordechai,
May God Bless You and Keep You
and the Lord Shine the Light of His Face Upon
You and Bestow Peace Unto You.

1995, Eight Years for the Kidnapping and Imprisonment of Mordechai
Vanunu

War is a Lousy Time

war is a lousy time
to quit smoking
war is a lousy time
for a toothache
war is a lousy time for
a woman dreaming
war is a lousy time
if you're not dead
war is a lousy time
to die all of a sudden
war is a lousy
time to live
war is a lousy time

Summer 1982

I Spit on You

To generals Sharon and Eitan

I could have easily killed there,
oh mother, this nightmare,
easily I could have killed
and what am I now, oh mother,
what would I be now if I killed
easily there. One less, oh mother,
oh, insane land,
one less me or
one less him,
let's say in a foreign alley,
there among the courtyards
within the walls
so easily...

Not me, not me, here I am —
I'm here to spit in your faces,
just go fuck yourselves,
you worthless bastards.

Fall 1982

Crying at the Movies

To Shelley

Now
between the wars
she cries well
in air conditioned movie theaters:

let the hero return to his lover
and carry her upon his arms,
the wind will blow through their hair
and she will extend her burning lips to him…

then this one will drop her popcorn cone
and begin to weep quietly

and I cry with her:
Once out of joy
(it's just a movie, remember)
and once out of terror –
how well she cries
between the wars.

After the Next World War

A poet shall not poetize
shall not sing
shall not even peep,
after the next world war.

III. Poems in Ashdodian

So You Won't Understand a Word

I write poems to you
in my Ashdodite tongue
kus em em emkum
(your mother's mother's cunt)
khla dar bukkum
(may your house come down on you)
so you won't understand a word.
Do you have a problem with that?
Who do you think you're?
Who cars about you?
Bustards!
One by one.
Why, when did you give a shit?
You who think you're this way
or that way,
you're so hip.

I write poems to you
in my Ashdodite tongue
so you won't understand.

Pathways to Heaven

There is no need to knock on the doors of Heaven Halls
in the town of Netivot.
There,
the bird on the light blue illustrated ceiling
looks like it's lost its consciousness and perhaps its soul,
to a targeted slingshot strike from a boy-sniper,
and any moment now she will fall down on the fish
which has also fainted, in my plate,
waiting for the lemon to come and refresh its fried spirit.
In Netivot's Heavens the Moroccan elders gaze wide-eyed
at the laser vision filled with might and terror and
a stifling scent of sulfur –
a pillar of fire and fireworks throughout and space music
and from within the smoke they see the voices
of "DJ Eyal Music" in a pretty good impression of the Lord on
Mount Sinai:
"And bind them for a sign upon your hand,
That they may be as frontlets between your eyes..."
And The People coughing and laughing, laughing and coughing,
and my mother, who looked for Gaza on the right the whole way
from Yad-Mordechai Says, such a shame we won't go by the Baba
Sali,
and I was stuck with Gaza to the right and my mother reminds me,
after the Six-Day we drove with you to Gaza, what a pretty market
like in Morocco,
we bought you a cage with birds that the soldiers confiscated at the
check-point
you cried the whole way to Ashdod about a cage with no birds.
And I amidst the smoke and laser beams wanted to tell her,
mother, the distance from here to Gaza is like that between us and
ourselves,
like an abyss within our heart, gaping like an ancient aching wound,
mother, the distance we walked here is like the distance of God in
the DJ's synthesizer,
like the distance of the bird from the ceiling to my plate now a pile
of fish bones,

like the distance of the birds from the cage, mother, and we are not
the birds in this parable, and we actually are the cage in this
parable, mother.

There is no need to knock on the doors of Heaven in Netivot,
the men and women have angel faces
and in their eyes the birds are still flying,
trapped as in a glass dream,
and only the tears are their blessing
to a distant beloved blue.

Notes:
Yad Mordechai is a Kibbutz, near Gaza, named after Mordechai
Anilevitch, the commander of the Warsaw Ghetto revolt.
Netivot is a little town in the southern part of Israel, populated mainly by
Moroccan Jewish immigrants.
Baba Sali is the Arabic nickname of the late Moroccan great Rabbi Yisrael
Abuhatzera, given to him by his hundreds of thousands of followers.
Baba Sali is today also the name of his tomb site in Netivot.

On The Way To 'Eyn Harod

On the way to *Eyn Harod**
I lost my trilled *resh*.

Afterwards I didn't feel
the loss of my guttural *'ayin*
and the breathy *het*
I inherited from my father
who himself picked it up
on his way to the Land.

On the way to 'Eyn Harod
I lost my *'ayin*.
I didn't really lose it –
Guess just swall'd it.

* (European Zionist "mayflower" kibbutz)

66

Ashdod Sugar Memory

And Ashdod is now an outlet
like the sea that she is herself
and how far to swim
and how much trust
in a shore with calm waters.

And Ashdod is now a memory:
at times the queen of dreams,
the courtyards of my grayish childhood
at times she is their death,
crashing against pre-constructed walls
the ghettos of my innocent childhood.
Like Madam Lugasi in the window
shaking her white head at me
from old age or the long sadness
and she knows how to count them all,
who had gone and what remained.

And Ashdod is a memory sweet sugar
that Mr. Lugasi – may he rest in peace –
used to <u>melt</u> into green and red lollypops,
or dip little apples in it
that we licked and nibbled for five *grush*.

And Ashdod is now an outlet.
Like a dream that she is herself.

These are the Names

And we had names with the scent of abroad:
Allén, venez à la maison, vite.
Jacquie, tl'a al-dar, d'aya.
And there was Beber with a triangle bod
and Pàtrick and Jojo and Dede.
The girls had names like bells:
Brigite, Alise, Michelle
Jorjette and Anette.

And the teacher wrote for us in her roster
our names in Hebrew:
Ilan, Ya'akov, Avraham,
David and Aliza, Zehava and Hanna.
Whatever… She thought she was gonna tell us.
We knew.
But we insisted
a bit more scent of abroad
before the ringing of bells is silenced:
Sami, Mimi,
Rachelle, Mardoshe…

My Eucalyptus Grove

The trees are twenty years taller
and the children are
the children of my childhood's children
who haven't yet learned how to sing rap
like in America,
and who still provide a living
for social workers,
counselors, parole officers and juvenile court judges,
for whom they built a courthouse of the peace
atop the hill amongst the trees
in the eucalyptus grove of my childhood,
to bring them in tiny handcuffs
before a peace loving judge
who was once the son of the grocery store,
poor man,
how with the pain can he not lose his mind,
or at least his judgment.

More Than Voices

In my childhood many played,
sounds of the West
and songs from Arabia.

But more than all,
more than their voices
rises in me the bone-piercing
melody of the voice
of uncle Binyamin

There in the magnificent feasts that my uncle vowed for years
in memory of the righteous Rabbi David Ben Baruch
in the small living room comfortably crowded
song and psaltery and scents of *Araq*
in the laughter of new immigrant jokes –
the desert generation.

Gone are the sounds of my childhood.
Gone too is uncle Binyamin.

On a screechy old record
Enrico Macias still sings:
J'AI QUITTÉ MON PAYS
J'AI QUITTÉ MON MAISON,
I left my country
I left my home.

Uncle Shimon is Dead

Uncle Shimon is Dead.
Uncle Shimon is Dead and with him died
a great piece of our soul.
Uncle Shimon is Dead.
We buried him at night after Shabbat
Between kodesh Le' hol
as you bury the righteous, and the moon
shone almost full revealing
the fallen faces of our beautiful women.
Uncle Shimon is Dead.
And the men as they carried him felt
how in spirit they too descend
another step into the hollow.
Uncle Shimon is Dead.
And I just cried.
Only later I got very frightened
How we are slowly orphaning.

Now as they read upon his grave *kaddish*
I recall an image from my infancy
in the Saharan oasis:
My uncle grilling meat over coals
and I kneel before him as cats do
to receive a tender little piece to chew.
One distant image,
distant now
like the distance of the *Maghreb* from the *Mashrek*,
like the distance of uncle Shimon from his grave growing full
dust to no return.

Grandpa Yihya

My grandpa Yehiel
they called him Yihya.
The distance between us is so and so
school years in the land of Israel,
so and so dust years
on the prayer book,
so and so psalms
so and so forgotten hymns.

My *dada* Yihya Lived and died in the Maghreb,
so and so hours of flight
from the land of Israel.
At times I run into him in Jerusalem:
White jalabah
black beret
hands crossed behind his back,
passing me by, innocently
not recognizing his image in me.

Even as a child, on the night of the seder
when my mother would rise to open her door
in honor of Elijah that he may come,
I would wish for him
for my grandpa Yihia.

Abu Shimon's Grocery

The bees used to make honey there
from the powdered sugar on the donuts.
Abu-Shimon, with the pride of a citrus tree,
would laugh and clap his hands together
and say: here, take one, don't be afraid.
Indeed the bees would take a short break
At the Turkish Delight
and the coconut rolls, blessed be.
After you've started eating the donut,
they would return to set in their tiny tubes
and joyfully extract. As if
Abu-Shimon's grocery existed
just for them, and they wouldn't wonder at all
when he would take out the bag of powdered sugar
(when no one was around)
and scatter some with his furrowed fingers
and laugh: here, eat, you little bustards.

Bus #18

When Madam Batito returns from the *souk*
she smiles at the world
from the open window of bus number eighteen,
wipes her sweat off with a handkerchief
and a juicy tomato with the sleeve of her dress,
lowers her eyes to the road to see,
bites, squirts, shakes a sheaf of Na'ana mint,
takes one big breath and sighs ahh.
She sets her eyes at the road to see
One good looking woman in one good looking car
smoking one good looking cigarette,
humming a song running a hand through her hair.
Madam Batito takes one long-long look,
adjust her baskets sighs ahh,
not out of jealousy she sighs ahh,
like a child looks at a bird sighs ahh
like smiling Madam Batito
from the open window of bus number eighteen
When she returns from the *souk* to her home.

Mother Tongue

My mother used to say
In French
Monsieur,
Madam.
And before that?
To a man she said *sidi*,
a woman they called *m'ra*,
in Moroccan.

My mother is now *g'veret*
in Hebrew.
For monsieur she says *adon*.

After the Opera

After the opera he will undo his tie
and wrap his body with a *jalabah*,
hand made by a craftsman
(special order from Morocco).
Then,
he will rinse his ears,
with the flowing streams
sweet streams of the *Oud*.

The World Didn't Give Birth to You, Son

Why are you breathing so heavily, son,
always carrying half the world on your shoulders,
Let them kill each other but you
come to mama you are not the world's son,
the world won't make you a cup of tea with *Na'ana*,
the world craps on you
my son,
crying for the ones your eyes have not seen
the miserable and the sick, the poor and the widow,
and what do they have to do with you
and what is your life,
smudging yourself for them like this
over entire newspapers
like black tears of ink.
Come, dear child,
they did not give birth to you,
I didn't raise you on yesterday's papers.
What do I ask?
Just sit here beside me.
Look,
a woman follows you restless
and your children call you to come,
come home, the world is not home,
No.
A man needs a home
my son
because the world is cruel and cold.

Why are you jumping and running around like this,
my son,
all over the face of the land,
from end to end
dragging with you the miserable, their piercing pain,
I know, my heart too is not made of stone.
It wasn't this harsh land that gave you life
and this land is a horrible riddle for you to solve. What are you?
Man, neither angel nor herald.
Look how tired are your eyes in midday

and what shall you say at night and what shall you dream my son?
Dream of a kind-hearted land,
but they have already walked away from you.
What are you laughing?
I no longer have strength to cry
and you too, breathing so heavily,
as if justice is breathing air. Go outside breath deeply,
there is no justice in the world,
my son,
there is jealousy, ill will there is, and hatred.
Justice is only in God,
my son,
and you are man, neither angel nor herald.
The Blessed-Be-He will do judgment with all,
and your prayer shall be silently answered.

Amen.

IV. A Distant Proverb

A Distant Proverb in Al-Arbiah Al-Mugrabia

Mother mother
New York is a distant city
and I grow distant within her.
Her towers raise in me yearnings for a balcony
and sea breeze, with tales over watermelon
to its last black seeds.
Mother mother
New York is a foreign city
And the Englizit lacerates longings in my soul
For a distant proverb in Mugrabi Arabic...

And how you used to rend me there:
Azhi a' yimma nurilk dar buk,
"Come mom, I'll show you your father's home."
Come mother and I'll discover America for you.

Contention

My heart is in the east
and I'm in the east,
my soul is in the east
and those loved by my soul,
those who want to take my soul
and my tongue
my mother's tongue,
all my songs
over there,
are sung
without me.

Here I am foreignness
here I am cutoff
I am a conflict
the heart is flesh
the heart from the flesh
the heart with the flesh.

Pure Honey from the Land of Israel

My father sends me from the Land of Israel
salted peanuts from *Giv'at Haim*
and citrus honey from *Yad Mordehai*
and I say to him: dad,
it wasn't because of hunger that I descended into Egypt.

Here I fill my belly
with hamburgers and hot-dogs
and train my lips in the local accent
like dad years ago
"A Minute of Hebrew" on government radio.
Years later, in front of the mirror, giving speeches
and we little ones giggle.
Union comrade
party comrade
everyone's comrade
and look,
your son says to you in proper Hebrew: dad,
it wasn't because of hunger that I descended into Egypt.
and your grandson pronounces his R like America,
and what's he got to do with the land of Israel?

New York

I need to train myself
to love this city,
I tell myself,
and the beggars nod to me
and extend a hungry hand to rip out my heart.
And the roads are gray with yellow spots,
like rattle snakes flowing whispering
to carry me in their endless coming.

And the glass towers reflect each other
and they have no opinion at all
of this city
indifferent to my need
to learn the love of the new
to make myself a home, here.
can I?

How can I
when in Jerusalem I left behind all my love
for beggars
for the stones
and my heart, robbed by
such hungry holy walls
in all their passion.

How can I
and I need to learn
to love myself
in this city.

New York, 1991

A Night of Scuds

When the scuds fell on Tel Aviv,
I went over to the Greek diner on the corner of Broadway.
The Greek served me American coffee,
but I didn't pick up on his being Greek
until he asked: Where are you from? You have an accent like…
You too I said.
He laughed, I'm from Greece, I'm already here twenty years.
We're neighbors, I told him.
From where? He asked.
The Middle East: I answered.
From the TV above his head the reporter from CNN
gave the first estimates of the damages in Tel Aviv
from a sealed room in Jerusalem,
and in the studio an American expert discussed
the deadly effects of mustard gas and nerve gas and I thought
of my mother and I remembered how shaken up she was at
the first air-raid siren during the '67 war, pulling
us kids along into the bomb shelter and whispering
prayers nonstop in Moroccan Arabic…
The Greek continued guessing in English: Jordan? Lebanon?
Yisrael, I said, in Hebrew.
you don't look Israeli, he said.
Depends, I told him.
He chuckled for some reason and added some hot coffee
to what was left cooling in my cup: Really,
you look more like an Arab.
On TV they were interviewing people on the street,
Israelis in the environs of sealed Tel Aviv,
and then I realized the Greek was right:
These Israelis are blond,
and they all speak perfect American English!
I thought I would write a sorrowful song,
but then I ordered a hamburger with lots of mustard.

The Gulf War, New York, 1991

The Plaza Fifty

Behold New York,
from the twenty-first floor of the Plaza Fifty Hotel.
It is easy to leave here and easy to stay
like that street-man down below,
would give the last piece of his coat
for one small glass of
a good vintage Cabernet.
I like Cabernet with
Brie over a wheat cracker
with green olives in garlic.
That's how I like my wine.
And the street-man goes to sleep now
inside the box of a
twenty seven inch Japanese television.
That's New York,
so easy to leave so easy to stay.

Fall 1985

At an Auditorium of a Local University

At an Auditorium of a Local University
Ammiel Alcalay (poet) reads an English translation
Of poems by Tikva Levi (poet).
I'm moved and aggravated –
When, for once, will our
Translated poems be able
To breathe in Hebrew?

New York, Winter 1991

Quick Take

In my poem you can't see
That I've got a green card
with an instant shot taken
at the Armenian place on
Salah ad-Dinn Street near
the American Consulate in
disintegrating Jerusalem.

In my poem you can't see
The irony in my eyes.

In my poems you can't see
the poetic limitation
of writing confined verse
In a country without borders.

In poems you can't see
deceitful art embroidering
hypocrisy, both essential
to my existence, just like
the mug shot from Salah
ad-Dinn Street on my
green card is now.

Homeland

Where is my homeland?
How well-worn a line to start a song of pain.
Where is home? Maybe that's better here, direct.
Come winter, I shovel snow from the stoop and as a child
The Saharan sun tanned my hide, mercilessly beating down.
So where's my homeland, ya'ani that place that is most mine?
Let's say, in Shami Israeli Arabic?
Let's say, in Shami Palestinian Hebrew?
My fingers stumble over an English keyboard,
Tripping and breaking to draw from my heart some shout or
murmur
That would be a slam dunk in Hebrew,
Tongue tripping onto tongue, language lapsing over lips.
So where? The hot lands are the cold lands too, now,
And the lovely bird (from Bialik's poem) now takes a shit on my
window
And she has no song and no story and I have no words to place in
her beak,
Ya'ani welcome back… no way, she's not into it at all.
Taking a crap on my head, crappy bird, fly, fly away, ya mal'ouna.
Where is that homeland? Biladi, biladi? Seriousness is what I ask
here.
Morocco's customs clerk greets me: marhaba bik fi-baldiq
Welcome in your homeland, this is no mistake, in your homeland!
And just a while ago they sent me a notice: come to vote
Maybe in my first democracy, who knows.
Morocco calls me back home; while the security woman at Ben
Gurion's airport
Always asks to hear my accent, my parents' names, my brothers,
my cousins… to get a clue…
When I lose my cool I say our names in Arabic: Sami, Yahya,
Zuhara, Yequt, Mayer…
In the U.S.A. the customs cop will ask: what was the purpose of
your visit to Morocco?
I returned on an El-Al flight from Israel; I point impatiently at the
arrivals hall.
Aha! He goes all detective on me, so what's a Moroccan doing in
Israel?

Aha, I go all academic at him, I wrote a whole Ph.D. about it, and
two hundred poems
And still don't have the faintest clue.
He gives up.
So where's my bayit? Al-bayt? Al-dar? La maison?
Home, fucking home!
I used to shake off that heavy-handed question with a glib response
- Home is my wife and children. Sometimes here and sometimes
there.
But now she's gone off to answer that selfsame question until she
fell into the arms of a Jewish American like her,
Ya'ani a Member Of the Tribe… and the children have scattered,
each one making a bit of a home for themselves until they come
back to search and dig into
Where is home? Where is my homeland? Where is my wife, that
member of the tribe? And where oh where is the tribe?
There was a moment.
There was one fleeting moment in Morocco where I almost found
it, I stood tall in djellaba and leather sandals,
Passing the time of day in that market of my childhood, traveling
among the villages of my infancy, etched deeper into me than
dozens of years in those damned projects blocks,
I could blend into them as into a magic mural I thought, and never
return,
The picture of my lost childhood, a Moroccan among Moroccans,
the son of a lost tribe, leaving only the telling.
Yes, there was a moment.
One long but fleeting moment
Like the embers of an abandoned campfire, stubbornly flickering…
And here, I have returned to Hebrew
To the homeland of my blindly Hebraic language
Is there another?
Lovely bird takes another crap.

(America, 4th of July 2011)

90

There Ain't No Nothing

I try on sandals in the old market of Errachidia,
town of my birth, that once was just called the market village
And now bears the name of the refugee camp,
Although it was named for Mulai Rachid.
But there's no coincidence and there ain't no nothing and nothing's
done.
I try on Italian sandals in the old market,
Two streets over from the house we used to live in, once,
Before we were reinvented as ignorant strangers,
And on the TV over my head Azmi Bishara
Speaks on Al Jazeera about Israel's intentions, hidden
And plain, and how I miss him now, here,
In the old market of the town of my birth, Errachidia,
Where there is not even one refugee to soothe the heart,
Nor even one gendarme, ya'ani border police, to break it.
I yield to the sadness that overpowers my bones
Like a man going under before a fateful surgery:
How is it that in this desert county, as big as the disputed holy land
Not even one Jew is left, all gone, and generally – there ain't no
nothing,
And I, as Moroccan as I know how to be, I know:
I'm at the tip of the Maghreb and my heart shreds in the Mashriq.

I Came Back From Morocco With A Certificate Of Birth

I came back from Morocco with a certificate of birth
And a cell phone that speaks Moroccan.
My birth certificate is a simple story, written in Arabic
On a page from a school-ruled notebook:
"In the fifteenth day in the month of May, nineteen hundred and
sixty
In Qasr Souk a man-child was born and named Sami, son of Meir
Chetrit, citizen of Morocco
Who was born in Gourma in nineteen hundred and thirty-seven,
a trader, and son of Yequt
Citizen of Morocco, born in Reech in nineteen hundred and forty.
Reported by the father on the twenty-seventh day of May, nineteen
hundred and sixty, and I, Abba Sidi son of Tahami, Qaid and
Registrar
I have signed this declaration after reading it to him."

The cell phone that I bought on a Meknes stopover on the way to
the desert of my childhood,
Filled up with the names of women and men:
Abdalhaq, Abdalrahman, Younes, Omar, Seivan, Vivian, Aziz,
Fairuz, Simone, Mina, Moustafa, Rabbab, Alcouhan, Bassidi, Nadir,
Jama'a, Muhammad, Lilian...
And my father, in a trans-Moroccan call said, lost in thought:
I think you've found yourself an old-new homeland between
America and Israel,
And now, it seems to me, you'll visit us even less.

Give Me One Moroccan King

Give me one Moroccan king,
A Moroccan with honor,
And take all your Bengurions, your Begins and Goldas,
Rabins, Shamirs, Pereses, Baraks and Sharons,
Go celebrate your sovereignty and independence with that lot.
I'll make do with a Moroccan king who speaks my mother's
tongue,
I'll bow my head and kiss his hand and swear allegiance to him
Allah yebrak fi mulai sidi
God bless my king
From now until the end of days.
Oh yes, indeed.
Why does this look odd to you?
Give me one Moroccan king,
A Moroccan man with honor,
Or at least a captain on a transatlantic flight
Who greets his passengers fluently in three languages, all with a
Moroccan accent,
And no one laughs (almost; my Jewish-American wife can't stop
herself.)

V. And Only Love

At the Crossroads in Winter

It's raining, take a break,
sit down,
take a sip from a cloudy breeze
calculate the days,
where will you lead the words?

where will they take you?

relax:
how many poems did you give birth to?
how many kids?
how many Sheqels?

and love.

It's raining, take a break,
don't say big words
about the stature of man.
Look at the raging rain
you are a dwarf, such a dwarf.

Look,
a crossroads in the winter.
Where would you lead the words
and where are you going with them.

Winter 1992

And Only Love

Sing
sing to me
sing to me again the same
sing to me again that same song
sing it again that song that you sang
that song you sang to me long ago when hair could stand against
the wind and my lips didn't wilt under the blue desert skies in your
eyes your voice like bells herds and herds of copper bell clappers
and gold and crystal the ringing of precious pearls
sing to me again that same song and do not say to me anything new
I'm tired of the new and the renewed my heart yearns for song
that song you sang to me once
of the deep skies of your eyes
sing it to me again
sing to me
sing
sing to me again
sing to me deceiving rhymes
for I am weary of the painful truth
I saw in your eyes still clear are the tears
a hundred years old or more streaming down your pure face down
over your breasts and your smooth belly that no man has known
I want to land on these plains that are eternal like the face of
the moon the age-old divine moon that did not know either small
steps or giant leaps for mankind that is choking now inside spools
and spools of optic fiber woven of false light
Sing to me and I will poetize for you now because I have seen
our light our light that we left in the enchanted ancient desert
when we were still naïve and innocent children
sing to me the ringing of bells
I'll rhyme you a medley
of slender rhymes
ancient
yours
mine
where are you
where are you now
and where is your rising poetry

I would burn all my thousands of words
to give birth to one divine note I am weary of man
I am weary and the man in me and in all is gloomy and naked
and pathetic mercy that I don't have it is not in my dwindled power
to create now from my squeezed heart drained almost if I would
not find it my virginal singing of bells and where are you today
whispering prayer in your hallucinated prayer houses
my miserable poetry will answer you with thanks halleluiah
halleluiah
Let the Lord open my lips but to you I shall cry out my song
awake awake wakeup my divine voice
for only our love
only love
remains
divine
remembrance
my compass
at sea
my heart
my ship
dark
circling
lost
and only love
now
searching
indarkness
shelter of the heart
like the poem
sing
me
a song.

1977 Innocence

On the night Begin took power
I was busy exploring the magical treasures
of one golden-haired girl
on a golden haystack.
I vote only for you,
whispered the sixteen-year-old girl
who didn't know right from left.
Only me, she knew that night.

In the morning we longed in our flesh
for the sweetness of the night,
the sun took the sky
and Begin* took the earth.

I had just turned seventeen,
All that's left is the scent of her hair,
yearning
and a poem.

* Menahem Begin, the right-wing Israeli leader. Took power and became
prime minister in May 1977.

ABOUT THE AUTHOR:

Sami Shalom Chetrit

Teacher, poet, writer, filmmaker, and scholar Sami Shalom Chetrit was born in Morocco, raised in Israel, and lives in New York City. He has been writing and publishing poetry for thirty years, with five books in Hebrew: a new book, *Broken Times*, is due out from Bimat Kedem (2014); this was preceded by *Yehudim* (Jews), from Nahar Books (2008). Chetrit's *Shirim BeAshdodit* (Poems in Ashdodian) became a bestseller in Israel where a popular musical, based on the poems, was produced. He has published countless poems in literary magazines, periodicals, newspapers, and anthologies, as well as several performing shows with leading Israeli musicians. There is a growing body of critical work on his poetry in both Hebrew and English and a generation of younger poets and artists have been inspired by his work. He was recently included in a list of the top 40 Modern Hebrew poets. Though a selection of his work appeared in Ammiel Alcalay's *Keys to the Garden*, this is Chetrit's first full-length book of poetry in English.

Chetrit's novel *Doll's Eye* came out from Hargol Am Oved in 2007, and in English from Xlibiris in 2013. His groundbreaking study, *Intra-Jewish Conflict in Israel: White Jews, Black Jews*, was published by Routledge in 2011.

Producer and director of three documentary films, Chetrit's latest film, Shattered Rhymes: The Life and Poetry of Erez Bitton, depicts the renowned Moroccan born poet, an inspiration to Chetrit's generation. The film came out in January, 2014, appearing in festivals as well as broadcast on Israeli television, and is available in English.

Chetrit is Associate Professor of Hebrew and Middle Eastern Studies at Queens College, CUNY, and is on the faculty of Middle East/Middle East in America Studies at The Graduate Center, CUNY.

ABOUT THE TRANSLATORS:

Ammiel Alcalay. Poet, novelist, translator, critic, and scholar Ammiel Alcalay teaches at Queens College and The Graduate Center, CUNY. His books include *After Jews and Arabs, Memories of Our Future, Islanders, and neither wit nor gold: from then*. His translations include *Sarajevo Blues* and *Nine Alexandrias* by Bosnian poet Semezdin Mehmedinović, as well as *Keys to the Garden*, an anthology of mizrahi writings translated from Hebrew and Arabic. A new book of essays, a little history, and a 10th anniversary edition of from the warring factions came out in 2013 from re:public/UpSet, both edited by Fred Dewey. He is the General Editor of Lost & Found: The CUNY Poetics Document Initiative, a series of student and guest edited archival texts emerging from the New American Poetry.

Poems translated by Ammiel Alcalay in this book:
Who Is A Jew And What Kind of A Jew He Is?
Hey Jeep, Hey Jeep
New Jerusalem
Acrid Memory
"And Thou Shalt Teach Them Diligently to They Children"
Victory Parade
Song of Ascent for Mordechai
So You Won't Understand a Word
On The Way To 'Eyn Harod
Ashdod Sugar Memory
These are the Names
My Eucalyptus Grove
More Than Voices
Grandpa Yihya
Abu Shimon's Grocery
Pure Honey from the Land of Israel
A Night of Scuds
At an Auditorium of a Local University
Quick Take

Dena Shunra is a translator of poetry and other matter, working with Hebrew and English, and studies Late Bronze Age Near East textiles, as reflected in myths spanning the lands between Sumer and Egypt.

Poema translated by Dena SHunra in this book:

I'm a Gotta Move Jew
A Mural With No Wall
My Mother Loves Arik Sharon
I am an Arab Refugee
Talking to an American Zionistomat
The Jew in Hebron
Speedy Jew
They can give it all back
A Man Seeks Roots
Red Kite
Thus Spake the Lord
An Answer for the Agents of Freedom
The Jews Are Killing the Savior
Sponja
Get Thee
Washing the Car
Measurements
In Lieu of Curses
We've Already Seen This Movie
Stupid Sheep in Sesame Sauce
Blessed Be She
Homeland
There Ain't No Nothing
I Came Back From Morocco With A Certificate Of Live Birth
Give Me One Moroccan King

Shay Y. Sayar is a PhD candidate for Comparative Literature, at the University of California Berkeley.
Poems translated by Shay Y. Sayar in this book:
My Love, My Land
Binding
Letter to the Bearers of the Dead
How Shall We Say Lo, How?
Midnight atop the Regional Garbage Dumpster
Like a Turtle
War is a Lousy Time
I Spit on You
Crying at the Movies
After the Next World War
Pathways to Heaven
Uncle Shimon is Dead
Bus #18
Mother Tongue
After the Opera
The World Didn't Give Birth to You, Son
A Distant Proverb in Al-Arbiah Al-Mugrabia
Contention
New York
The Plaza Fifty
At the Crossroads in Winter
And Only Love
There is Something of the Divine in this Business
1977 Innocence

ABOUT THE EDITOR:

Fred Dewey is a writer, teacher, and editor. His book The School of Public Life (errant bodies/doormats, 2014) explores building public space and neighborhood councils in Los Angeles. He was director of Beyond Baroque Literary/Arts Center from 1996 to 2010 and designed, edited, and published twenty books, including work by Simone Forti and Ammiel Alcalay. He has taught at the Otto Suhr Institute of the Free University in Berlin and is on the graduate fine art faculty of ArtCenter College of Design in Pasadena, CA.

www.ingramcontent.com/pod-product-compliance
Lightning Source LLC
Chambersburg PA
CBHW030949090426
42737CB00007B/559